ORC WARFARE

Rosen
YA
New York

Chris Pramas

This edition published in 2018 by
The Rosen Publishing Group, Inc.
29 East 21st Street
New York, NY 10010

Cataloging-in-Publication Data

Names: Pramas, Chris.
Title: Orc warfare / Chris Pramas.
Description: New York : Rosen YA, 2018. | Series: Creature warfare | Includes glossary and index. | Audience: Grades 7–12.
Identifiers: ISBN 9781508176244 (library bound)
Subjects: LCSH: Animals, Mythical—Juvenile literature. | Monsters—Juvenile literature. | War in literature.
Classification: LCC GR825.P73 2018 | DDC 398'.45—dc23

Manufactured in China

This edition published by Rosen Publishing by arrangement with Osprey Publishing, an imprint of Bloomsbury Plc.

CONTENTS

CHAPTER ONE:
THE ORCS

This chapter introduces the orc race. It discusses their physique and breeds, and the many branches of orc kind that have spread across worlds. Chapter 1 also includes an overview of orc society, the anatomy of an orc horde, the difference between a warchief and a warlord, and details on shamanism and magic.

CHAPTER TWO:
ORC TROOP TYPES

Orcs can field many different types of troops, from common warrior infantry to the rarely seen Flesh Eaters. This chapter catalogs the troops of orcs and some of their allies, and covers their basic tactical uses in the field.

CHAPTER THREE:
ORC STRATEGIES AND TACTICS

Orcs have tactics? Indeed they do, and this chapter talks about them in some detail. The various tactical roles of troops are discussed, along with specific strategies and tactics. The focus is on field battles, but there are also sections on siege warfare and naval tactics.

CHAPTER FOUR:
ORC VICTORIES

Analysis is all well and good but Chapter 4 is where we can see it all in practice. Orc Victories details four battles and one siege that show how orcs fight. It wouldn't be a proper military book without war stories and here they are.

That brings *Orc Warfare* to a close, but not the story of the orcs. That, as ever, marches on.

INTRODUCTION

To use the word orc 100 years ago was to invite confusion. There were malicious faeries and spirits from folklore and mythology to be sure, but nothing quite like the orc. It began, as many fantasy staples did, with *The Lord of the Rings*. J. R. R. Tolkien set the template of the orc in modern fantasy. In his tales orcs are twisted, evil creatures – the foot soldiers of dark lords like Morgoth and Sauron. Their numbers seem endless, but they can be cowardly when confronted or when their leaders are slain.

From Tolkien, orcs spread to the role playing game *Dungeons & Dragons*, where they became pig-faced beast-men. And from thousands of readers and thousands of gamers, orcs spread to countless fantasy worlds. Now orcs are a go-to ingredient of modern fantasy, along with elves and dwarves. They are in books, games, and hugely popular movies. If you say the word orc today, many people will nod along. Yes, orcs, of course. They have become part of our culture.

It is therefore not as strange as it might appear that a publisher known for its extensive line of historical and military books, would commission a book about orcs. Why not take orcs, the scourge of a thousand worlds, and give them a military and cultural analysis? Why not take a fantasy race and give it the proper treatment? *Orc Warfare*, the book you hold in your hands, attempts to do just that. The book is broken down into four chapters.

THE ORCS

We were made for battle. The Smite-Father blessed us with strength and fury, the War-Mother with cunning and fortitude. When our horde is on the march, elves hide in their trees and dwarves in their caves. Their pathetic gods cannot protect them.

Trimbul, Orc Shaman

Orcs are a common threat across many worlds. Nowhere do they live in peace. Orcs do not farm. They do not write poetry. Orcs raid and fight and kill. When they are not attacking other races, they fight amongst themselves. No orc wants to grow old and soft. A good orc death comes in battle, surrounded by the corpses of enemies. That is the orc way.

Orc tribes have many, often contradictory origin stories for their race, but they all share some common points. Foremost among them is the idea that the gods of the so-called civilized races (dwarves, elves, and humans) sought to cheat the orc gods of their due. This sets up the basic dynamic of the orcs and their enemies. The civilized races are hypocrites and it is up to the orcs to take what is theirs with fire and sword. And what is theirs, according to the orc shamans? Everything!

ORC PHYSIQUE

There are three breeds of orcs: goblins, common orcs, and great orcs. Most tribes feature a mix of all three, though it is not unknown for there to be tribes of strictly one type.

Goblins (also known as lesser orcs) are the smallest. They have spindly frames and range from 4 to 5ft in height. As bigger orcs often bully them, goblins are the most likely to strike out and form tribes of their own. Roughly 25 percent of all orcs are goblins.

Common orcs are more muscular and range in height from 5 to 6ft. They make up the majority of the orc race. So much so that few bother to say "common orc" when talking about them. They are simply orcs. Roughly 65 percent of all orcs are common orcs.

Great orcs are over 6 ft. in height and monstrous. They are the toughest and fiercest members of their race. In orc culture size and strength bring status.

Thus great orcs lead and dominate most warbands. Roughly 10 percent of all orcs are great orcs.

Orcs of all breeds are ridiculously fecund. They reproduce at a rate that cannot be matched, or even approached, by their enemies. The implications of this in orc warfare are explored in the 'Warband and Horde' section later in this chapter.

Orcs are also notable for their diet. They are meat eaters. Indeed, they eat nothing else. They can consume the meat of nearly any creature. When they cannot find another source of meat, they eat each other. Goblins being the weakest, they are the first to go into the stewpot.

The shamans say that the gods bred orcs for war. Certainly no one doubts their ferocity in battle. It does not end there though. Orcs may die in battle, but they yet serve the tribe and warband. Orcs do not have funerary customs as other races understand them. Rather, the corpses of the dead are broken down for further use, starting with flesh for the hungry. Their guts can be made into bowstrings and their bones sharpened into arrow tips. Their heads can also be turned into horrific weapons (see War Machines in Chapter 2). The shamans can make no sense of burying or burning the dead as other races do. Warriors should serve the tribe, in life and in death.

ORCISH SOCIETY

Orcs are a nomadic people. They must move from place to place to find fresh sources of meat. They rarely stay in the same area for more than a few weeks, except during the winter months. While camped, they engage in two main activities: hunting and raiding. The hunts are focused on big creatures like aurochs and bears, as well as mammoths when they can be found. While the hunts are dangerous, they provide great sport for the orcs and meat in large amounts when successful. Raids are launched against nearby enemies (including other orc tribes) on a regular basis. They too provide meat, but also other things the tribe needs: weapons, tools, alcohol, and shiny objects. Orcs have a particular love of raiding trading caravans that are foolish enough to go through their territory. They are easy prey for orc warbands and fat prizes.

Orcs favor terrain that works best with their nomadic lifestyle. This is why orc tribes are most common on the steppes and plains on the outskirts of civilization. Here the tribes and their wolves and chariots can roam free. Orcs are highly adaptable, however, and over the millennia they have spread to the far corners of many worlds. While the focus of this book is on the orcs of the steppes, the following section includes some details about differing orc tribes.

Desert Orcs

The desert suits the nomadic spirit of the orcs quite well. Their main difficulty was finding a suitable mount, as the horses favored by the human tribes were repelled by the orcs' smell. The answer was the orgilla, a species of giant lizard the orcs found and domesticated. This black and yellow striped beast thrives in the desert and its poisonous bite is deadly. Now the desert orc tribes are fully mounted on orgillas and they roam the harsh landscape at will. Armies tend to be small in the desert, as there just aren't the resources to support troops in large numbers.

Desert orc tribes roam from oasis to oasis. Since water is more precious than gold in the desert, it is the cause of most battles there. The orcs fight human nomads most often, as both groups have similar lifestyles and needs.

Forest Orcs

Orcs rarely populate the great forests. Wood elves and giant spiders alike hunt them there, and the terrain is totally unsuitable for chariots. Nonetheless, some orc tribes learn to survive in this environment. They do so by adopting the guerrilla tactics of their elven enemies. They operate in small groups and strike from ambush. They attack quickly and disappear back into the brush. A scarce few tribes make deals with the giant spiders, luring prey their way in exchange for the spinning of webs that obscure orc camps.

Forest orcs have little cavalry. It is not well-suited for navigating the often thick undergrowth of the deep forest. They have become expert climbers, however. Goblins in particular excel at scaling the tallest of trees speedily. This allows the orcs to launch ambushes from high above their foes and then disappear into the forest canopy.

Hill Orcs

Hill orcs are a weird aberration, at least according to other orcs. They build things! Forts are their specialty. They have also learned to throw up

fortifications quickly. Hill orcs on the march in enemy territory put up a walled camp by dawn every day. They are not exactly nomadic but neither are they sedentary. They build a series of wooden hill forts, and lightly garrison each one. The main part of each hill orc warband moves from fort to fort, hunting and raiding in that area while using the fort as a base. When pickings dry up, they move on to the next one. Other orcs think they must have some dwarf blood in them, but it is not wise to suggest this to a hill orc's face.

Since hill orcs maintain a network of forts, they make greater use of war machines than others of their kind. Each hill fort maintains at least a half-dozen ballista and a smaller number of catapults. Their ramparts are also well-stocked with stones that can be hurled down upon attacking enemies. A few keep large cauldrons above the gate. Scalding water from these can be dumped on attackers trying to knock down the gates. They do not use oil for this because their forts are made of wood. Scalding is just as effective at disabling enemies.

Jungle Orcs

The jungle orcs claim that they were the original orcs. The War-Mother, so they say, birthed the orc race into the hot embrace of the jungle. Many orc tribes left this home, driven away by its heat and poisonous denizens. Not so the jungle orcs. They claim that only they follow the old ways. Armor is unknown to them. They only wield weapons of wood, bone, and stone. Their darts and javelins are covered in poison. Like the forest orcs, they are masters of stealth and ambush. Few have tried to conquer their jungle home. Those who tried have regretted it.

Some tribes of jungle orcs live on the bones of the ancient civilization of the serpentmen, long since fallen. They build new dwellings in the ruins and scavenge what they can from the pyramids of the dead. The serpentmen of today, though degenerate and lacking the sorcerous power of their ancestors, fight the jungle orcs fiercely for their birthright.

Mountain Orcs

Mountain orcs are more squatters than nomads. They delve beneath the great peaks and occupy the caverns and cities they find there. Sometimes these are the wreckage of ancient and long dead civilizations. More often than not, they encroach on dwarf lands, and the fighting between the two races is bitter. Mountain orcs are the only members of their race that can be said to have cities, although these were conquered instead of being built. Even here, however, the orcs are never content with their victories. Always they push further and deeper, scouting and raiding the tunnels that worm under the mountains.

Mountain orc hordes do not, for obvious reasons, feature cavalry. Battles underground are the purview of infantry. Furthermore, goblins do well in this environment. They can squeeze through tunnels that other orcs (and even dwarves) cannot.

Sea Orcs

Orcs are not, it must be said, the best of sailors. Nonetheless, there are those orcs who spend their lives on the sea. This began as an act of desperation. Orcs chased to the coasts with no other way out captured ships and took to the water. It was rough going at first. The orcs had no traditions of seamanship and navigation, but they could follow the coast and at least keep themselves afloat. Many drowned in the early days. The ships of other races killed more. The survivors hung on though and they came to realize something. The orcish ways of fast movement and lightning raids could be just as effective on water as on land. This was the birth of a scourge that now haunts many lands: orc pirates.

Sea orcs live much like their steppe roaming brethren. They have winter camps but few permanent settlements. They prefer to keep on the move, traveling up and down the coasts looking for ships and towns to raid. They do build their own ships, but these are crude things. They prefer to capture ships from their enemies. Sea orcs favor galleys, since they can be powered by brute strength (something orcs have in abundance).

As with others of their kind, sea orcs use numbers to their advantage, and this is why their ships rarely travel alone. Instead, pirate flotillas ply the sea lanes. These are motley affairs, with ships of all sorts pressed into service. Coastal settlements live in fear of the orc pirates and for good reason.

Swamp Orcs

Few orc tribes end up in the swamp by choice. Victorious enemies usually drove them there, and they had to adapt or die. They fought long wars with the native lizardmen, who did not take kindly to the orc invaders. This feud continues to the present day and raids between the two races are common. The swamp orcs do not have the swimming ability of their opponents, but they have developed into skilled boatmen. Their expert use of flat-bottomed boats gives them a mobility enemies in this environment do not expect.

Swamp orcs raid the surrounding countryside regularly and then fade back into the swamp with their booty. From time to time local lords send troops to root them out of their boggy homes, but this rarely ends well for the invaders. The swamp is inhospitable at the best of times and the orcs' mastery of the terrain gives them the advantage. The swamp orcs have humbled armies many times their size.

Tundra Orcs

Tundra orcs live in bleak and frozen lands. While all orcs hunt, tundra orcs do it to the exclusion of nearly anything else. The raiding that is so common on the steppes does not feature much in the tundra. There simply aren't that many tribes there, orc or otherwise. Great white wolves are their constant allies, and this enables them to hunt the largest of creatures. Every tundra orc dreams of bringing down one of the mighty wyrms that lair in the wastelands. To be a wyrm-slayer is the highest of honors.

Humans sometimes set up whaling stations along the coast. While such places are usually walled and well-defended, the tundra orcs take their existence as a challenge to their territory and do whatever it takes to destroy them. Whale meat and oil are both valuable commodities for the orcs.

WARBAND AND HORDE

When the civilized races fight the orcs, they see little organization in their enemies. It is not surprising that soldiers accustomed to uniformed armies in serried ranks would see it so, but orcs do organize for war. Their enemies just have a hard time discerning it.

The basic orcish tactical unit is the warband. This consists of a warchief and his followers, usually from the same tribe. Generally speaking, a warband is made up of 25 to 200 orcs. Sometimes a warband represents all the fighters from a tribe, but this isn't always the case. A large tribe may include several warbands, and some warchiefs attract orcs from several different tribes. While tribal identity is important to orcs, in battle the status of the warband is pre-eminent. Orcs want to follow powerful and successful battle leaders and being a part of a famous warband is an honor.

An orc army, known as a horde, forms when a warlord who can command the loyalty of many warbands emerges. As has been noted, orcs are a fractious lot and warbands fight against each other at least as often as they fight enemies like elves and dwarves. A warchief who wins battles against rival warchiefs and external enemies can rise and become a warlord. Eventually, warbands will come to join the warlord of their own free will. When a horde forms, it means big battles are ahead and all orcs want a part in that.

Curse of the War-Mother: An Orc Myth

In the earliest days the gods fought a war against the titans for the possession of the worlds. The gods of the humans, dwarves, and elves came to the Smite-Father and War-Mother and asked for their aid. "We need mighty warriors," they said. "If you fight by our side, we will share our bounty with the orcs forever after."

The War-Mother was cautious; she did not trust these gods. The Smite-Father was tempted by a battle against the toughest of foes, so he agreed to aid the gods. The war was long but in the end the gods triumphed. The Smite-Father defeated the titan's champion in single combat, ensuring their defeat.

After the final victory, the gods held a great feast. The god of wine was ever at the Smite-Father's side, filling his horn after every sip. Exhausted by battle and drunk on wine, the Smite-Father slept. It was then the gods gathered to divide the spoils of the war. They intended to cheat the orcs of their due, but they had not reckoned on the War-Mother.

She of the Baleful Eyes burst upon their secret council. "We fought by your side and this is how you repay us?" she thundered. "You call yourselves civilized but you are nothing but liars and thieves. You don't want to share the spoils of war with us? So be it. The orcs will take it from you, in war after war, down through the ages. Prepare yourselves — the orcs are coming for you!"

And so it was and ever shall be.

The Rising Horde

A horde is the personal expression of an orc warlord. Left to their own devices, orc tribes would continue their nomadic cycle of movement, hunting and raiding. It takes a powerful personality to fuse disparate warbands together to make an army. A warlord by definition is an orc with the brutality and cunning to come out on top of hundreds of confrontations, both physical and political. Due to their natural gifts, great orcs are usually the warlords. This is not always the case, however, and even goblin warlords are not unknown. All warlords have advisers, though they are not always listened to! Most of them are famous warchiefs from the horde. Shamans are also well-respected and can always give their opinion.

Once a warlord raises a horde, it must be pointed at a target or it will fall apart. Thousands of orcs cannot sit idle for too long or they will simply begin fighting amongst themselves again. A savvy warlord knows that a horde not in use will not be a horde for long. It is thus often the case that by the time civilized lands even understand that there is a threat brewing, a horde invasion of their territory will already have begun.

The warlord decides the target of the horde's attack. He may treat the whole thing as a giant raid whose primary purpose is meat and plunder. There is usually more to it than that. Orcs have been fighting the nations

of dwarves, elves, and men for centuries, so there are always reasons to go to war. Some warlords are out for revenge and others for glory. Some want nothing more than to write their name in blood in the annals of orc kind. Though it may not be obvious, every warlord has a motivation. Wise enemy commanders try to understand what it is and use this knowledge in their strategies of defense.

Sworn Warlords

As has been discussed, orcs respect size and strength. Warlords, while proud and fearsome in their own right, are not immune to these feelings. Sometimes even the toughest warlords realize that there are leaders more powerful than them. These warlords swear their hordes into service and thus become part of something even greater.

What sort of leader can command the respect of an orc warlord? They can be generally categorized as "dark lords." They can be mighty sorcerers, champions of demon princes, powerful undead, or ruthless emperors. They are enemies of civilization and they are always in need of savage soldiers. Orcs make perfect additions to their armies.

Sworn warlords hope to increase their own power and status. This is rarely good news for orcs under their command. Dark lords place little value on the lives of their servants. Orc hordes are thus used as cannon fodder more often than not. Dark lords do not care if one hundred tribes are wiped out assaulting a high elf fortress. They can always find replacements.

SHAMANS AND MAGIC

Shamans are important leaders in orc tribes. They are intermediates between the gods and spirits and the orc people. They provide counsel to warlords and warchiefs. They maintain the history and stories and teach them to the young. They act as judges and make most of the important day-to-day decisions for the tribes, except for war (battle, of course, is the purview of warlords and warchiefs). For all these reasons and more, shamans are deeply respected in orc society. It is their mastery of magic that makes them feared, however. Orcs know that to cross a shaman is to invite a curse or worse. Warlords and warchiefs want the shamans' magic on their side when battle comes.

Orc magic is not flashy. Shamans do not shoot lightning from their hands or cause the earth to swallow their enemies. They are, however, expert alchemists and practitioners of spirit magic. Their magic aids orc tribes in many ways, but we will concentrate here on the role of magic in orc warfare.

Alchemy is used to create two fearsome weapons: war-heads and fire-shot. These are described in more detail in Chapter 2. Shamans also use alchemy to make a variety of potions and salves. Since these are created in small batches with often rare ingredients, they are usually given to warlords, warchiefs, or other champions. The most common potion makes the imbiber stronger and faster for about an hour, but then wickedly hungover for several hours after. Proper use thus requires careful timing. Before big battles, shamans will often coat a warlord's whole body in a salve that helps protect it from cuts and blows. This does not make the warlord immune to damage, though many act as if it does once the fighting begins.

More potent magic is done with the aid of spirits. Shamans summon and bargain with such spirits to achieve a variety of effects. First, they are able to inflict curses. This is done by sending spirits of mischief to plague enemies. These are usually minor spirits, so the curse seems like a run of bad luck to the recipient. They find themselves tripping at inopportune moments, or they have weapons slip from their hands in battle. More powerful spirits can have direct effects, like causing blindness or lameness.

Shamans achieve their most potent effects by spirit binding. By the use of long and exacting rituals, they can summon powerful spirits and bind them into items – usually weapons or armor. This is how shamans create magical items. They can create flaming weapons by binding fire spirits into swords or axes, for example, or make armor extremely resilient by binding an earth spirit to it. Some shamans go down a darker path and bind demons instead. This can create more powerful magic items, but summoning demons is much more dangerous. They are more difficult to bargain with and they always try to trick their summoners.

ORC ARMOR AND WEAPONS

The nomadic lifestyle of the orcs does not lend itself to the forging of metal. There is some activity of this sort during winter camp, but they have nothing to match the forges of the dwarves in their mighty cities. They thus get most of their metal weapons and armor by trading with other tribes or looting defeated enemies. While they may not forge the metal, orc craftsmen do customize everything. Equipment is re-sized, painted, decorated with fetishes, and carved with orc script. A dwarf axe in orc hands for just a few days becomes all but unrecognizable.

One skill orcs do have is tanning. Their great hunts often bag animals whose hides can be cured to make shields and armor. This is why leather is the most common armor in a horde. Helms too can be made of leather and sometimes the skulls of large creatures. Luckier orcs have metal armor looted from the battlefield. Chainmail is the most common, and it is often collected in pieces. An orc might get a hauberk in one battle, leggings in another, and so on. Later pieces of plate may be added. This gives the orcs a motley appearance, with no two orcs looking exactly alike.

Since metal is hard to come by, wargear is considered an asset of the tribe. When orcs die, their armor and weapons go back into a common pool used to equip the tribe's warriors. This is in keeping with the way orcs treat the bodies of the fallen. Everything is a resource for the tribe's survival. Burying perfectly good weapons and armor? That's the sort of crazy thing only dwarves and humans do.

The favored melee weapons of orcs are scimitars, spears, and axes, in both one- and two-handed varieties. Swords of all sorts are common as well, most of them looted from various battlefields. Orcs prefer scimitars, which suit their wild slashing attacks better than straight blades. Some warriors prefer to use great cleavers in combat, which is perhaps not surprising in a culture that butchers as much meat as the orcs. Select tribes have developed skill in the use of the man catcher, a pole arm with curved prongs that can loop over an opponent's head and drag them to the ground. It is effective against cavalry, pulling riders from their mounts, and can be used to capture prisoners.

Ranged weapons of choice are javelins and bows and they are by far the most common. Some tribes, notably those of the hill orcs, favor the sling over the bow. Other orcs used looted crossbows, but they are not skilled in maintaining them (particularly the mechanically complex dwarf models). In siege situations orcs sometimes use pitch to make flaming missiles. They are used to light buildings on fire and cause panic. Flaming missiles are much less accurate but that matters little when shooting at large structures.

ORC TROOP TYPES

The warlord of an orc horde has many troop types under his command, from common orc infantry to wolf-riding goblins to mighty trolls. Some troop types are rarer than others, and few hordes feature them all. The following chapter breaks down the component parts of an orc horde and looks at each in detail.

WARRIOR INFANTRY

Orc warriors have reach, strength, and ferocity. We have skill and discipline. Both are required to defeat them.

Fornir, Dwarf Veteran

Common orc warriors make up the largest part of any horde. They are available in numbers, easily motivated to fight, and possess some skill in individual combat. Warrior infantry are melee troops, usually armed with spears, swords, or axes. They typically wear leather or chainmail armor and carry shields. Some prefer two-handed weapons, axes in particular.

Orc warriors are not known for their discipline. They don't fight in formation as their opponents do. A warband of such troops resembles a mob more than it does a military unit. Warrior infantry relies on ferocity and intimidation to carry the day. Formed troops that don't panic and weather that first wild charge will usually triumph over orc warriors. If their line breaks or their troops panic, however, then the orcs are in their element. Orc warriors in these situations excel at causing terror and then taking advantage when the enemy suffers a total collapse of morale. Battles can go from closely run contests to absolute routs in a matter of minutes.

BERSERKERS

The elves say the berserkers are cursed but they have it backwards. They are blessed. The spirit of the Smite-Father possesses them and they perform deeds worthy of him on the battlefield.

Trimbul, Orc Shaman

On the eve of important battles, some orcs go through a frightening transformation. A madness descends on them. They tear off their armor and howl like beasts. According to the shamans, the spirit of the Smite-Father infuses them. These berserkers are considered blessed but also dangerous. Some lose their minds completely, so bloodthirsty that they attack their comrades before the real battle can be joined. To forestall this, shamans will throw prisoners in with the berserkers. These unfortunates are quickly torn to pieces. The berserkers then go into battle caked with their blood.

Berserkers are all but impossible to control. A warlord cannot deploy them when and where he desires. They seek the enemy out as soon as they can. At best they can be sent forward in small groups so they have more impact. The presence of even a few berserkers can be felt, however. When they charge forward, axes and cleavers whirling, screaming out the Smite-Father's name, many enemies will flee rather than face them. While most berserkers will die in the ensuing melee, they can cause casualties and disruption out of all proportion to their numbers.

Those few that survive a battle face an uncertain fate. Some regain their faculties. They can remember what they did during the glorious time they bore the blessing of the Smite-Father, but they are lucid enough to return to the tribe. For others the madness never ends. These the shamans feed drugged meat that will keep them unconscious until the time of the next battle is nigh. Those that cannot be controlled in this way are cut loose from the tribe and left to wander alone until their minds return or death takes them.

IRONBACKS

Ironbacks, form up! We are marching straight up their gullet and by the War-Mother, they will choke on us!

Cragnak, Orc Warlord

Warlords in some orc hordes form greater orcs into units of shock infantry known as Ironbacks. They are armored from head to foot in either scale or plate armor. They carry tower shields and spears and, unlike other orcs, they fight in formation. Orc generals use Ironbacks to punch through enemy battle lines, disorganizing the foe so orc warriors can pour in after them and finish the job. While many would say that orc faces are ugly enough, Ironbacks often wear full-faced helms with masks depicting demons and other hideous monsters.

The trouble with Ironbacks is that it takes time to form them up and deploy them on the battlefield. They have the discipline it takes for this maneuver, but the same cannot be said for other warbands in the horde. It happens frequently that warrior infantry surges forward to attack while the Ironbacks are still forming up. It takes a skilled warlord to hold the horde back so the Ironbacks can strike the first blow.

SKIRMISHERS

We shook out a skirmish line but it could not hold against the orcs. It seemed there were three of them for every one of us, and their javelins filled the air.

Valan, Human Soldier

The first weapon a young orc is trained to fight with is the javelin. They spend countless hours learning to aim and throw javelins before they ever get near a sword or an axe. When young orcs first go to war, it is as skirmishers. Speed is prized, so they wear little armor (leather at best). Each carries a bundle of javelins and a short sword or hand axe. Skirmishers range ahead of the warrior infantry, finding and fixing the enemy. Their job is not to engage troops but to harass their battle lines with volleys of javelins and then beat a retreat, only to roll forward and do it again. This keeps the enemy busy while the rest of the orc horde comes up and readies for battle.

Many skirmishers who survive this bloody baptism of fire later join the warrior infantry. Others train with the bow and become scouts. Goblins in particular favor bows, as they are not as fast as their larger brethren and the bow allows them to attack from further away. Some goblin warbands form their archers up so they can concentrate their fire. Such warbands are usually deployed on the flanks for the horde and used for supporting fire. A small number of orc tribes have mastered the crossbow and prefer it over the bow.

SCOUTS

The human guards were drunk and expected no attack. We slit their throats and opened the gates. After that it was just slaughter.

Roguz, Orc Scout

Scouts are older orcs with years of experience in skirmishing, tracking, and reconnaissance. In most warbands their numbers are small and they do most of their work before the battle begins. While they sometimes use giant wolves to travel at speed, they dismount when they get into their operating area and do their real work on foot. This lets them make the most of cover and concealment. Some of the most effective scouts are actually half-orcs who can pass for human. They can walk right in to human settlements and gather intelligence without attracting undue attention.

Scouts have two main roles in an orc warband or horde. First, they observe and analyze the enemy, providing the intelligence the orc leaders need to make combat decisions. Second, they operate as infiltrators, stealthily silencing guards, starting fires, and causing other distractions that their comrades can take advantage of. Once the main engagement begins, scouts take advantage of the chaos to either withdraw or compound the confusion by assassinating enemy officers and messengers. A small group of scouts can thus have an outsized effect on a larger battle.

GOBLIN BUSHWACKERS

Captain Slorvic chased the orcs into the forest and we followed. Sergeant Janos urged caution but Slorvic's blood was up. We chased shadows in that forest until goblin knives were in our backs.

Kris, Human Mercenary

Warfare on the steppes tends to be two-dimensional. This is not the case in other types of terrain, however. In the forests, swamps, and mountains, fighting can happen in all three dimensions and this is where goblin bushwackers come into play. These goblins are excellent climbers and they can scramble up walls and trees with amazing speed. They use this ability to set up ambushes on unwary foes.

Some goblin bushwackers like to use javelins. They can hang with one arm and throw javelins with the other. Certainly a shower of javelins from above is a rude surprise for any army. Carrying javelins can be cumbersome, however, so most bushwackers prefer to use short blades and daggers. In this kind of ambush, they let the enemy get below them before attacking. Then they leap from above, daggers out, and stab their enemies as they fall. This is, of course, a dangerous maneuver. If seen, they can be impaled on spears and lances, or simply evaded before they can attack. When executed with surprise and skill, though, a bushwacker attack can be deadly. One minute the forest is quiet, the next goblins with sharp knives are falling from the trees!

Once the bushwackers have made their attack, they do not stick around. They wear little armor and know what will happen to them in a stand-up fight. They attack, cause as much mayhem as they can, and then climb into cover and try to disappear. Such an attack can be over in less than a minute but leave dozens of dead and wounded.

WOLF ARCHERS

They are breaking! Scimitars out – now we ride. Our wolves will feast on flesh tonight!

Marguz, Goblin Wolf Archer

The bond between orcs and giant wolves is ancient and strong. When the Smite-Father and War-Mother go to battle, it is said they ride on the son and daughter of the Lord of Wolves. If there was ever a time when orcs and giant wolves were not allies, history has not recorded it.

Goblins are the most numerous riders of giant wolves. Their size makes them ideal for this, as does their affinity with the bow. Wolf archers are the eyes and ears of the orc horde. They fan out ahead and to the flanks, seeking the enemy and also trying to neutralize their scouts. When an orc horde invades hostile territory, wolf archers also act as terror troops. They slip between armies, burning villages and attacking supply lines. Then they use their speed to escape pursuit.

Wolf archers are lightly armored, wearing leather at best. They do not carry shields, as they need both hands for their bows. They carry scimitars for close-in work, though they try to avoid it until the enemy runs away. In battle wolf archers have a support role, using archery to pick off exposed targets until the opposition breaks. When that happens, the wolves are unleashed and they mercilessly pursue the fleeing enemy.

WOLF SPEARMEN

The scouts had sent their ammunition wagon up in flames. When the dwarf crossbowmen ran out of bolts, I sent Vargabeg and his wolf spearmen to destroy them. Not one dwarf survived that charge.

Argitan, Orc Warlord

In some hordes the burliest of the giant wolves are given orc riders and used as melee troops. The orcs wear chainmail, carry shields, and wield long spears and scimitars. They leave the scouting to the wolf archers, as their role is that of shock cavalry. A canny warlord holds them in reserve and then commits them when a weak point in the enemy battle line is found. Their mobility means that they can get to any point on the battlefield quickly, and exploit opportunities warrior infantry or Ironbacks would miss.

The charge of the wolf spearman is brutal. First their long spears strike home, sending enemy troops sprawling. Then the giant wolves are among them, snapping and tearing with their sharp teeth. Finally the orcs draw their scimitars and lay about them. Such a charge has broken many a battle line. They cannot, however, go toe-to-toe with the heavy cavalry of the humans and the elves. The large, barded horses and heavily armored riders simply outclass the wolf spearmen. For this reason they usually evade such foes, which the speed of their wolves allows them to do in most situations.

FLESH EATERS

By the gods, what were those things? Those horses ate our dead! What unholy magic could create such abominations?

Peledor, Templar Knight

The name Flesh Eaters does not refer to the orcs, as it goes without saying that they eat flesh. No, the sobriquet is that of the horses that they ride. Normal horses want nothing to do with orcs. They find the smell of orc-kind revolting and react violently to any attempt to ride them. Even goblin wolf riders, who are practically born in the saddle, find no purchase on the backs of horses.

The Flesh Eaters were the answer to this problem. Several tribes of orcs spent decades breeding and warping horses with the aid of shamanic magic. The end result was a frightening horse that shared the orc diet: meat and nothing but. These horses are horrific in appearance—gaunt but with a mouth of sharp teeth—but orcs can ride them. Furthermore, the Flesh Eaters are trained for war. They trample and bite enemy soldiers in combat. When the battle is over, they feed on the wounded and dead.

As yet only a few tribes have Flesh Eaters. They have used them to field true heavy cavalry that can answer the knights of human armies. Great orcs in plate armor ride the Flesh Eaters into battle. They are shock cavalry like the wolf spearmen, but even harder hitting.

LIGHT CHARIOTS

What could we do? Those chariots rode circles around the caravan, shooting arrows at anything that moved. When the guard captain fell dead, I took his horse and rode for my life.

Abdur, Caravan Guard

Some tribes continue to uses chariots in their warbands, a practice with a long and storied history in orc warfare. The majority of them are light chariots pulled by two giant wolves. The crew of such a vehicle consists of a driver and a bowman, frequently but not always goblins. The chariot provides a stable platform for archery that also has great mobility. Warlords use them to deliver focused fire on troublesome parts of the enemy battle line. Orc leaders also make use of light chariots for their own transport in the field. This allows them to get to critical sections of the battle quickly. It also makes them easily visible to their own troops and is thus good for morale.

One advantage of light chariots is that they can be disassembled easily for portage. On many occasions orc hordes have crossed mountains or rivers with chariots on their backs, only to reassemble them in the clear terrain beyond. This is often a rude surprise to their enemies.

HEAVY CHARIOTS

The charge of those chariots was grim enough. They smashed into our line, trampling and scything men down. Then we saw the orc warlord himself was in the lead chariot. He was over seven feet tall and he wielded a huge spear with deadly skill. No one could stand against him that day.

Sir Janosy, Prince Korbert's Lifeguard

Light chariots have many uses, but crashing into enemy battle lines is not one of them. That is a job for the heavy chariot, a larger and more imposing version of its speedy cousin. Heavy chariots have a crew of four and are pulled by four giant wolves. They have sturdy sides meant to protect the warriors in battle. Many also sport scythes on their wheels, which cause great carnage when used on closely-packed enemy troops. A typical crew consists of one driver, two spearmen, and one archer. Since it is rare to see heavy chariots in large numbers, their missile fire is more annoyance than threat. Their true value is in the charge. Disciplined troops with proper training know how to deal with them (open up lanes for the chariots to move through), but such troops are few and far between. It is far more common for opponents to either panic and run before they strike home, or be broken by the terrific impact of a heavy chariot charge.

Great orcs are particularly fond of heavy chariots. Their long reach is an advantage when fighting from such a platform, and they use them with devastating effect. Many orc leaders prefer to command and fight from heavy chariots as well. They believe these hulking machines of death send the right message to friend and foe alike!

FIRE-SHOT TEAMS

Fire-shot teams to the front. I want that village to burn!

Gorgamar, Orc Warchief

Some shamans know the secret magic to create the Blood of the War-Mother, an alchemical liquid that explodes if touched by the smallest spark. It is volatile and dangerous but orcs delight in the mayhem it can cause. When a shaman makes a batch of Blood of the War-Mother, small amounts are sealed into a section of intestine (orc or animal, whatever is available) that looks something like a sausage. This in turn is enclosed in a wooden or metal sphere small enough for an orc to throw, which is further enchanted by the shaman to spark when struck with sufficient force. The resulting device is called a fire-shot. In battle an orc throws a fire-shot hard and fast. When it strikes something—an enemy or a hard piece of terrain—the magical spark ignites the Blood of the War-Mother and creates a fiery explosion. They are deadly when thrown into a tight formation of troops or fortifications.

Carrying fire-shots is, of course, dangerous business. Incoming missile fire can cause them to explode, as can melee attacks from troops who don't know any better. Sometimes it takes nothing more than a hard fall to cause the fire-shots to explode. Life expectancy among fire-shot troops is not high and yet there is never a lack of volunteers.

To minimize accidental detonation, fire-shot troops are organized into teams of three orcs. One orc carries a tower shield, which he uses to provide cover to himself and the shot carrier. The latter orc carries a supply of fire-shots, usually about a dozen. The third orc in the team is the thrower and he carries his own shield for missile defense. These troops are recruited from the best javelin throwers and they can toss fire-shots accurately up to 50 yards (45.7 m).

Fire-shot teams usually move up with the skirmishers right before an assault. They go in single file, shield-bearer first, shot carrier next, and shot thrower in the rear. When they get within range, the shield-bearer plants the tower shield, and the carrier hands the thrower a fire-shot. The thrower can either lob the fire-shot from behind the tower shield or move to the side under cover of his own shield and throw from there. Throwing from behind the tower shield is safer, but moving to the side makes the shots more accurate.

Experienced orc fighters know what fire-shots can do and they fear the Blood of the War-Mother. Some will send out small bands of melee troops, even though they know it could turn into a suicide mission. Other armies have had success with sling-armed skirmishers. They can get around the tower shield and pelt the carrier with stones until a fire-shot explodes and takes care of the problem. Orcs try to defend against this with their own skirmishers, and this often leads to fierce fighting between the battle lines.

ORC PIRATES

While the foot sloggers are throwing themselves against the walls, we're going to sail into the harbor and take the city by surprise. We'll loot it and be gone before our cousins fight their way in!

Captain Bullitt, Orc Pirate

Orc pirates are the scourge of the coastal settlements and their deadly attacks are much feared. Pirate flotillas tend to operate independently, but on occasion one will ally with a land-based orc warlord. This happens when their interests align. For example, when both a warlord and a pirate flotilla want to sack the same city and neither has the strength to do it alone.

Orc pirates excel at boarding actions against enemy ships and surprise raids. They provide two great assets to land-based warlords. First, they can launch attacks from the sea or up navigable rivers that a typical horde cannot. Second, they can use their ships to ferry other troops where they are least expected. The pirates' pride is touchy, and loading other orcs onto their ships can be a time-consuming affair due to the scuffles that inevitably break out between land and sea orcs. The speed of the ships is considered worth the trouble.

Warlords who ally with their seaborne brethren soon realize that orc pirates will not be fighting in any set piece battles. That is not their way. They are raiders and fight as such. Orc pirates rarely wear armor, as metal armor at sea can be a death sentence. They favor short weapons like cutlasses and hand axes that won't get fouled in the rigging. Bows are popular, as are crossbows when they can get them. Some ships carry fire-shots but they are not popular with orc pirates. Even leaving aside the danger of lighting one's own ship on fire, the pirates prefer to capture other ships rather than destroy them. That's how pirate flotillas grow.

WAR MACHINES

Orc war machines are crude affairs that are as likely to hurt them as us. The war-heads you have to watch out for though. They are as dangerous as they are repulsive.

Rorik, Dwarf Engineer

With their nomadic lifestyle, orcs do not make a great use of war machines with but two exceptions. The first is the ballista, which is essentially a giant crossbow that takes two crewmen to operate. These weapons fire large bolts—spears really—that can punch through the toughest armor. Orcs often mount ballista on wagons to give them at least some mobility. The wagon also ensures the ballista has a good supply of ammunition on hand.

Ballista can fire more than bolts. In fact, they deliver the most gruesome of all orc weapons, the war-head. Long ago, shamans discovered they could take orc heads and turn them into weapons. They perform a magical ritual on the heads of the dead and then seal each one in a small barrel full of alchemical fluids. Ballista can launch the resulting war-heads at the enemy with horrific results. When the barrels land, their contents explode and create a cloud of choking green gas. War-heads are used to break up enemy formations and cause panic. The gas dissipates in less than a minute, but those who breathe it are incapacitated by coughing fits for up to an hour. Plenty of time for an orc charge to hit the now compromised enemy formation.

In siege situations orcs sometimes build catapults as well. These are crude machines that require a dozen crew or more, engineering not being an orc strong suit. These war machines fling huge stones at enemy fortifications in the hopes of creating a gap the horde can assault through. They also can hurl war-heads over walls to cause mayhem within. Whereas a ballista can

only shoot one war-head at a time, a catapult can throw them in bunches. They are tied together loosely so the barrels will scatter while in the air. This is, of course, wildly inaccurate and it is not uncommon for war-heads to land among friendly troops when fired in this way.

TROLLS

Kruzz crush! Kruzz kill!

Kruzz, Troll

Trolls are huge, savage monsters that stand over 10ft tall. They live in caves in small groups and roam the surrounding area for food and loot. They happily feed on orcs – and just about anything else that crosses their path – but they are not without intelligence. Sometimes orc warlords can lure the trolls out of their caves and entice them to join a horde. If food has been scare in the region, the promise of fresh meat is often enough to get the trolls to march to war.

In battle trolls are a nightmare. They are enormously strong and they wield giant clubs and axes to deadly effect. Their skin is naturally tough and can often deflect blows on its own. Trolls become even more fearsome when armored. They are sometimes given huge tower shields and sent forward with orcs behind them. They provide cover for the orcs and then smash open the enemy formations.

The weakness of trolls is that they have even less discipline than orcs. After slaughtering an enemy unit, they will stop to eat and plunder. The warlord may desperately need them for another charge, but the trolls will not be moved before they are ready.

DARK MINIONS

The Crimson Knights and the Free Companies will march to war with the orcs. So let it be said, so let it be done.

Valberna, High Priestess of the Crimson Banner

Orc hordes, particularly when led by sworn warlords, often fight alongside the armies of dark lords. Such forces include human warriors seduced by the dark lord's promises. They have many names, but for the purposes of this book we will refer to them as dark minions. As troops they run the gamut from ill-trained conscripts to elite knights. The fodder is of little account and usually dies quickly on campaign in any case. The core of the dark minions is made up of hard-bitten professional soldiers, often ex-mercenaries, who want to be on the winning side, no matter how distasteful it is. Some are fanatical cultists, true believers in their dark lord.

These human soldiers do not, as a rule, like orcs and for good reason. They likely have fought against orc hordes on numerous occasions. Soldiers who serve a dark lord, however, get used to following orders, so orcs and dark minions fight side by side when so commanded. Orc leaders remain wary, however, as the captains of the dark minions are a treacherous lot. Given the opportunity, they will let the orcs bleed for an objective and then try to take the credit. There are, of course, exceptions. Sometimes orcs and dark minions fight well together and develop tactics to take advantage of their disparate skills.

HELLMOUNTS

That devil beast ignored the king entirely and instead focused its wrath on the court astrologer. That's the only reason the king escaped, though they don't mention that in the songs.

Gerardus, Bodyguard of King Trienko

It is said that hellmounts are demons from beyond the mortal plane. They look like huge black horses, but they have little in common with equines. They snort fire from their nostrils and can even breathe fire in battle. Hellmounts are intelligent and cruel, though their motives are often a mystery. Long ago certain orc shamans made pacts with hellmount bloodlines. When a horde gathers, they sometimes arrive to aid their orc allies. Always there is a price. Usually, the orcs must seek and kill specific individuals. Why these people in particular must die is never explained.

Hellmounts never appear in large numbers. An entire horde may have half a dozen of them. The most exalted warlords and warchiefs ride them into battle. There their flailing hooves and gouts of flame strike terror into the enemy.

MONSTERS

They've got a yeti! Heat that oil faster!

Kaino, Station Captain

Some orc tribes have developed a tradition of monster handling. Dealing with such creatures is dangerous work, but many warlords find it worth the risk. Monster handlers use a variety of techniques. Some communicate with the beasts and make simple deals with them (usually involving food). Others use goads and torches to get the monsters to do their will. In either case these monsters are usually short-term allies at best. The longer they are with a horde, the more likely they are to rampage at an inopportune moment.

Orcs use whatever monsters they can get and these can vary widely. Swamp orcs make use of native giant alligators, particularly when on the defense. Forest and mountain orcs use giant spiders when they can. Tundra orcs are known to bring yeti to battle, albeit rarely. Regardless of the monster, the basic tactics are the same. The handlers send the monsters at the enemy and then retreat once battle is joined. There is no chance of controlling such beasts once they are in combat. Orc leaders simply try to take advantage of the chaos they create as best they can!

ORC STRATEGIES AND TACTICS

There are no orc tactics manuals or war colleges. They do grow up hearing stories of their tribes from the shamans, and these tales do include some tactical lessons. For the most part, however, orcs learn war by practicing it. What orc warlords do by feel and instinct is what leaders of the civilized races spend lifetimes trying to master.

This chapter discusses orc strategies and tactics. The treatment is, by necessity, quite general. There are many factors that can affect battles, from weather to supply shortages to command rivalries, and no treatise can take everything into account. Nonetheless, there are many common features of orc warfare that can be analyzed and this is what follows.

ORC STRATEGIES

Orc strategies are built around two things: speed and terror.

An orc horde can march like no other army. The slow moving wagon trains of other armies do not exist in a horde. Everything is designed for speed of march and speed of attack. The expectation is that the horde will find food on the go. If it does not, a horde can survive for some time eating its own without affecting its combat strength too much. An orc horde can march up to 30 miles a day and even after such a march they are capable of fighting battles. Their enemies call them "foot cavalry" for this reason. Forces made up entirely of cavalry can go even farther in a day.

A horde on the march does not travel as one compact mass; it is too difficult to feed that way. Instead, a warlord usually splits the horde into three or four columns that travel in parallel into enemy territory. The warlord leads one column and his trusted warchiefs the others. There is usually 5–10 miles between columns. This gives each one room to find supplies but is close enough that the horde can concentrate when the enemy is near.

The columns are also an important part of the orc strategy of terror. A horde is already a large force, but the use of columns on the march makes it seem even larger. When a horde advances on a front up to 40 miles wide, it makes their numbers seem endless. All of a sudden, orcs seem to be everywhere. Warbands of wolf archers roam forward and to the flanks, finding and burning villages, but always letting some enemies escape. Warlords want these refugees to flee ahead of the horde, spreading harrowing tales of fire and blood and so causing panic. They know that if they can instill terror in the enemy before the armies clash, winning a victory will be that much easier.

The wolf archers are key troops to the orc advance. They keep the columns in communication as they move. They find settlements to raid for food. They also keep tabs on the enemy formations. They can spot when the enemy is divided in the face of the horde. This often allows orcs to concentrate two or three columns on an isolated enemy force and crush it before it can be reinforced. The horde is potentially vulnerable to this itself when split into columns, but they are notoriously difficult to catch.

The speed of the orc columns can also be used to wrong-foot an advancing enemy. Columns can, and often do, simply converge on the enemy when they come on. Orcs, however, rarely need to worry about defending a base area. This is not true of their enemies. Thus warlords often have their columns converge behind advancing foes, thus putting themselves between the enemy army and its base of operation (be it camp, fortress, town, or city). Now the enemy is cut off from supply and reinforcement and must turn itself around. The orcs can pick the field they want to fight on, and they have the option of sacking the enemy base as well. A maneuver like this also damages enemy morale before a single blow is struck.

BATTLEFIELD ROLES

The previous chapter detailed many different types of orc troops. Few hordes feature them all. Orc tactics are built around battlefield roles, and these can be filled by different troop types depending on what a warlord has available. The primary tactical roles are:

Reconnaissance: This role is usually performed by scouts and wolf archers. If they are not available, skirmishers can take it on. They are the eyes and ears of the horde.

Pinning: Many orc tactics revolve around pinning an enemy in place once they are discovered. The job of the pinning troops is to prevent the enemy from slipping away while the rest of the horde moves up. Skirmishers take on this role in nearly every horde. Light chariots are also used for pinning.

Breakthrough: Every warlord needs a force that can punch through the enemy battle line. Ironbacks, heavy chariots, wolf spearmen, Flesh Eaters, and trolls are all shock troops that can break nearly any enemy if employed correctly.

Follow-up: Once a breakthrough is achieved, there is still hard fighting to do. This is the classic role of the warrior infantry. They plunge into the hole created by the breakthrough, and widen and expand it.

Exploitation: When the enemy breaks and begins to flee, fast-moving troops are needed to follow and attack them. This not only kills more of the enemy, but also makes sure they keep running. Wolf archers and wolf spearmen (if not previously deployed) most commonly take on this role. Light chariots are also sometimes used. If none of these are available, it falls on the warrior infantry to finish the job.

Support: Throughout the battle, missile fire can provide support for both offensive and defensive moves. Formed units of archers, often goblins, are the most common support troops. Ballistas are excellent support when available.

Again, hordes don't necessarily have access to all the troop types they need. Often warlords must make do with what they have, or give troops different roles at different times in the battle. Since warrior infantry outnumbers all the other troop types by far, it is often they who are called upon to do what must be done when other troops are not available.

RAIDING TACTICS

I hired a mercenary band with good references to guard a caravan. Brothers of the Forge, they called themselves. They turned out to be bodyguards from the northern cities. They didn't know the first thing about fighting orcs. There were no survivors.

Malik, Human Caravan Master

The most common form of orc warfare is raiding. Hordes only gather once in a while; raiding happens all the time. It is usually a single warband that goes raiding, though sometimes several gather together to attack a particularly juicy target. Raiding forces generally number between 25 and 300 orcs. More than that and they can get unwieldy. Raids are meant to be quickly organized and executed.

The Orc Charge

You never forget your first orc charge. The noise of it is just indescribable. And the way they yell – you feel it in your bones. I pissed my britches, I can tell you that, but I stayed in formation and survived. Many men from my village did not.

Callum, Human Mercenary

Elven and dwarven leaders claim that the charge is the only tactic the orcs know. This is not true, but it is the case that the charge is the first tactic employed in most battles. This is not because the orc leaders are dimwitted but because it succeeds more than it fails. After countless generations of war, orcs know that aggression wins battles. The army that attacks first – and with confidence – is often the army that carries the day. This is why orc warbands are so quick to engage. They understand a quick, sharp blow is often all it takes to decide the issue.

The charge itself is a savage thing. The warbands gather around their warchiefs, while horns blare and drums beat. Then the mass moves towards the enemy, standards held high. The orcs scream and shout battle cries and bang their weapons on their shields. They do not advance in ranks, but as a wild and frenzied mob. The fact that orcs usually outnumber their enemies only adds to the impression that the charge is unstoppable. That intimidation is exactly what the orcs want. They want the defenders to doubt themselves and their leaders. They want them to know fear. For any foe of orckind, the moments before the first charge are crucial ones. Those that master themselves and stand firm have a chance of weathering the charge and fighting the orcs off. Those whose courage fails them break and flee before contact. That means a battle becomes a rout before the first blows are even struck. Orcs love nothing better than hacking down fleeing and demoralized foes, and this is why the charge is their favorite tactic.

Most raids are launched for three reasons: plunder, food, and intimidation. Some are done for revenge, particularly if the warband itself was raided recently. Typical targets are caravans, villages, and camps of rival warbands. The first task is to locate inviting targets. This falls to the scouts, though sometimes locations are well known from previous raids. It is also the job of the scouts to examine the defenses and look for areas of weakness. All this information is brought back to the warchief, who decides if a raid is taking place and how the approach is to be made.

The key to a successful raid is surprise. For this reason many warchiefs make their approach during the night, attacking at dawn at the latest. Scouts move in first, cutting the throats of any guards and opening the way

for the main attack. They signal the warchief with an animal whistle and then the warband leaps into action. The orcs use surprise and numbers to neutralize any opposition before it can come together. Potential centers of resistance (like guard barracks) are hammered first. After that, they turn their attention to the attack's main objectives.

Most raids are over in less than an hour. The warband sweeps in, crushes resistance, and then takes what it came for. Plunder, food, and prisoners are quickly gathered and then the warband is off again. Some wolf riders like to pull prisoners behind them on the way back to camp. They call this "tenderizing the meat."

BATTLEFIELD TACTICS

When hordes gather, raiding continues but now the orcs can take on larger foes in bigger battles. Orcs, as discussed later in the chapter, are not enthusiastic practitioners of siege warfare. They always prefer a short, decisive engagement to a long, drawn out siege. Hordes seek out field battles, for these are their forte.

Pin and Flank

We hit the elves so hard their trees back home fell over.

Lorbul, Orc Warchief

Pin and flank is a classic orc tactic that takes advantage of their speed. Once the scouts or wolf archers have found an enemy force, the skirmishers are sent ahead to pin them in place. This doesn't mean that the enemy becomes immobile. Rather, they are likely to pause and deploy for battle once skirmishers are dashing in and out of range and peppering them with javelins. If the skirmishers find that the opposition is already deployed, their job is to push in the enemy's light troops so their commander knows as little as possible about what the orcs are up to.

Most hordes have a mobile strike force. Wolf archers and spearmen are most common, but some warbands have light chariots or Flesh Eaters as well. While the skirmishers keep the enemy's main force busy, this mobile element swings wide and tries to flank. Flanking being a common tactic to all armies, they may well run into their opposite number while on the move. These cavalry actions can become battles in themselves. If all goes well, the flanking force arrives back on the field once the two battle lines have engaged. They then launch a charge to the flank, or even better, the rear. Such attacks strike panic in most soldiers, allowing the flankers to roll up the enemy battle line. Few enemies can come back after a blow such as this.

Since the orcs are fast marchers, this same tactic is used with infantry when terrain permits. Forest orcs, for example, are known for quick flank marches through the hidden ways of their homeland. Then they burst upon the enemy from an unexpected quarter and suddenly it seems that orcs are everywhere.

The Spear Thrust

Stand firm, men of Boros. I'll take the troll leader!

Last words of Tibor, Paladin of St Cuthbert

A wild orc charge can, as we've seen, often carry the day. Against well-disciplined enemies, however, a general advance like that can be contained and driven back. Dwarven and elven spearmen have long experience in just this sort of warfare, and they can deal with orcs many times their own number if their line holds. Flank attacks can unhinge them but these are not always possible. Sometimes there are no flanks to turn. Other times the flank force is parried and deflected away.

In these situations an orc warlord has no choice but to crack the battle line open. Orcs liken this to attacking a man in a breastplate. You can slash at the breastplate all day with a sword and never penetrate it. A sharp spear with enough force behind it will punch right through the breastplate and into the soft meat behind. That is what this tactic tries to achieve.

First, the warlord must find the weakest part of the enemy's battle line. If there isn't one, it is up to the support troops to make one by bombarding a section of the battle line with arrows and war-heads (if the horde has ballistas). Then the warlord must choose his spear. These are the best shock troops available. Ironbacks do the job admirably if they have time to deploy. Heavy chariots strike fear into the enemy as they charge forward with scythed blades. Orcs mounted on Flesh Eaters surprise and shock the enemy. Wolf spearmen move fast and hit hard. Trolls are nigh unstoppable.

The chosen shock troops launch their assault on the weakened enemy line, followed up and supported by warrior infantry. Sometimes the spear can be blunted or knocked aside by heavy missile fire or a counter charge. If it strikes home, however, it is a rare battle line that can stand firm against the impact. The shock troops punch through the enemy and go deep into their now exposed formations. The warrior infantry comes right behind, making the hole bigger and spreading panic. As long as the warlord continues to feed in new troops and support the spear thrust, the enemy's defeat is a foregone conclusion.

Mobile Defense
How do orcs defend? By attacking!

Readuth, Dwarf Tactician

While orcs rarely need to hold ground for its own sake, there are circumstances under which they must defend an area (they are in winter camp, for example). Sworn warlords are sometimes tasked with defending a line of fortifications, a river crossing, or suchlike. While orcs can certainly fight behind defenses, it is not their preferred way of war. They would rather mount a mobile defense in such situations instead.

A dwarf army that had to hold a line would turtle up and defend the front line with their main force, perhaps keeping a few troops in reserve. Orcs essentially do the opposite of this. Their front line defenders are few in number and consist mainly of missile troops and skirmishers. They can do the required patrolling and raiding but their numbers are not enough to blunt a sustained attack. The bulk of the orc force, divided up into columns if defending a large region, remain back from the front line. They wait until the enemy commits himself in force. The archers and skirmishers fall back, giving up ground that can be retaken later if necessary. Then the columns move up to take on the enemy.

Feigned Flight
The orcs cannot run forever. Soon we will bring them to battle and end this threat once and for all!

King Marjan, Monarch of Anvari (deceased)

When orcs are attacked by superior forces, many of their traditional tactics become invalid. Some warlords fight anyway and are defeated. Others cut and run, and look for easier prey. Cannier warlords try a third option: lure and strike.

In this tactic the horde seems like it is retreating, but it does not use its usual speed. It pulls back slowly, staying just ahead of the enemy and fighting sharp engagements with units that probe ahead. The warlord wants the enemy general to believe that he has a chance to catch the horde and defeat it wholesale. In reality the warlord is simply biding his time, pulling the enemy further and further from his base of supplies. Ideally, the enemy army is lured into terrain that the orcs like and can exploit to their advantage. Then the warlord picks the spot where the horde will turn and strike. The chosen battlefield has features that favor the horde. This may be as simple as terrain features that secure the flanks (a river or a swamp, for example). The best spots allow the orcs to spring a large-scale ambush and completely turn the tables on the pursuers.

Once the enemy army is away from its support and in the right spot, the warlord turns the horde to strike. The long march and constant fighting should have taken its toll on the enemy army. They may be running low on supplies. The soldiers are likely frustrated that they can't seem to catch the orcs. They long for a decisive fight. Suddenly, it's upon them and not in the way they wanted. The army that was retreating is now on the attack. Orc columns may appear behind them, cutting their route back home. Armies without strong leadership or discipline often crumble in this situation. Then the orcs become the pursuers, hounding them as they try to retreat. More than one army that felt it was on the verge of victory has been destroyed in a matter of hours by the use of lure and strike tactics.

SIEGE TACTICS

Orcs do not like sieges. They take too long. They involve long periods of boredom. They nullify the orcs' speed, which is one of their great advantages in the field. It is unsurprising then that the orcs never developed a tradition of military engineering. This, of course, puts them at a disadvantage in sieges, which only serves to reinforce orc thinking on the subject! Like it or not, there are times when sieges become inevitable. Dwarves love to hunker down behind fortifications and use their deadly war machines. Humans have their cities with wall after wall. ("What kind of coward needs seven walls to hide behind?" the orcs ask.) When an enemy buttons up inside a fortified city or castle, what is an orc warlord to do?

Escalade

That wall is the only thing standing between you and victory. One hard fight, boys, and then fresh meat for the stewpots!

Tilligor, Orc Warchief

The first thing any orc warlord will try is mounting an escalade. This is an attempt to use siege ladders to get troops up and over the wall so the orcs can get to slaughtering. Some hordes use battering rams as well and attack the gates simultaneously. Most other races consider an escalade a risky maneuver with a high cost in casualties that should only be attempted after a garrison has been weakened by hunger and disease. Orcs would rather go right into the teeth of the enemy defenses than wait around for better conditions.

If materials are available, they can knock together some ladders in a day or so. More aggressive warlords will just send the infantry at the walls and try to bull through. Seasoned warlords at least try to cover the approach of the assaulting warbands with missile fire from archers and ballistas. Since the defenders are behind fortifications, this fire is unlikely to cause many casualties. Its goal is to keep the defenders in cover, however, so the warbands can move up without losing too many troops.

Once the assault warbands get to the walls, the real struggle begins. The orcs must climb the ladders and fight their way onto the battlements. Meanwhile, defenders will be firing arrows and other missiles at them and attempting to push the ladders down. Defenders have been known to throw nearly anything, from daggers to rocks to buckets, to try to dislodge those climbing the ladders. Many fortifications heat oil or water in cauldrons that can be poured down on the attackers. It's a brutal business that inevitably leaves hundreds of corpses at the bottom of the wall. If the orcs can gain a lodgment on the walls, however, it is often the beginning of the end for the besieged. No one wants orc warbands on the loose in city streets.

Reduction

No one is mining under the walls. The orcs are nomads. They don't know the first thing about it.

Autarch Pindos, Commander of Libakis

A more orcish tactic to reduce fortifications is undermining the walls. There are some orcs, most notably the mountain orcs, who are excellent tunnelers. If the fortifications are not built directly on rock, they can tunnel under the walls to destabilize them. Such a tunnel is built with wooden supports so it does not cave in prematurely. At the right time, the end of the tunnel is stuffed with combustible material and set alight. This burns away the supports and hopefully sends the wall crashing down.

Undermining is a dangerous operation and it too takes time. First, there are the natural dangers of digging any tunnel. Then there is the possibility of detection. If the defenders realize what's going on, they can dig counter mines. If they find the orc tunnels with one of their own, they can send raiding parties down to attack the mine and wreck the tunnel. Many savage battles have been fought in the dark of the tunnels, invisible to the world above.

A few warlords have come up with ingenious ways to reduce a fortress. In one famous incident a warlord had his troops dig a new channel for a nearby river. The original path of the river was dammed and then the new route opened. This sent the water hurtling towards the walls of the fortress. The constant flow of water undermined the foundations of the walls and compromised the defenses. This ruined the fortress for further use, but the orcs did not care. They were never going to keep it anyway.

Cooperation

"My men will take down the gates. Your orcs will be the first through it."

Krohne the Conqueror to Warlord Verak at the Siege of Petrik

Orcs may not be great at sieges, but warlords usually at least understand their shortcomings. While many prefer to go it alone in battle, a siege is one situation in which warlords are genuinely happy to have help. The sworn warlords have a real advantage here, that they are part of something larger. Dark lords usually have at least some troops with skill in military engineering. This makes the orcs' jobs much easier.

When fighting with allies, the orcs can leave the engineering to those who do it better. Dark lords can often provide more advanced war machines and equipment. Siege towers are a better way for orc infantry to assault a wall than ladders. Trebuchets can hurl larger stones than orc catapults. Fire throwers can burn the defenders out of a tower in seconds.

One thing orcs do not like about fighting with allies is that their commanders often want to starve out the garrison. While this is a sensible tactic that weakens the defenders, the orcs see it differently. They, of course, plan to eat the defenders once they break into the fortress or city and starving people do not make a good meal. Orcs don't want something scrawny and stringy as a reward for a battle won. They've likely had enough goblin over the course of the siege!

NAVAL TACTICS

Sea orcs are not large in numbers compared to their land-bound cousins, but they have managed to survive and even thrive on the water when few thought they could. As mentioned in Chapter 1, sea orcs operate in pirate flotillas. This is essentially the waterborne equivalent of an orc horde. Since orcs are not great builders of ships, flotillas are mostly made up of captured vessels. While they are decorated and made to look suitably orcish, a flotilla is a mishmash of ships of different styles and sizes. Orcs prefer galleys, as they are excellent rowers, but they take whatever ships they can capture. Due to the nature of pirate flotillas, naval tactics are limited compared to those of other races.

Boarding
If that ship burns, I'll tear your heart out!
Captain Grethe, Orc Pirate

The go-to tactic of all pirate flotillas is the boarding action. It is the one best suited to the orc temperament and capturing ships is how flotillas expand. Orc ships carry more crew than typical human and elven ships, so they can bring superior numbers to bear when attacking. Orcs love a short, sharp boarding action that provides loot, fresh meat, and a new ship for the flotilla.

The main problem sea orc ships have is actually catching their prey. Orcs are still not great sailors and their ships – heavy with pirates – are often slow. It thus requires some ingenuity on the orcs' part to catch enemy ships. Since flotillas have many ships at their disposal, one favored tactic is to set up a cordon of ships in one area and then have another group of ships drive the enemy towards it. If timed right, this traps the enemy ship and eventually at least one orc ship will be able to board it. Once that happens, more ships from the flotilla can come up and send their pirates into the fray. It is a rare ship that escapes once caught in this trap.

Raiding
Orc ships sighted! Militiamen, to your posts!
Mirko, Watch Captain

It didn't take orc pirates long to realize that raiding coastal settlements was easier than chasing down ships. A village or town isn't going anywhere after all! It is thus a common tactic of orc flotillas to cruise up and down the coast looking for good targets to raid. These flotillas range over a wide area, as it was learned that attacking the same settlements again and again led to diminishing returns.

Pirate flotillas prefer night attacks on coastal settlements. This allows them to come in under the cover of darkness and gain the element of surprise. It also means there is unlikely to be pursuit when they sail away. As with their nomadic cousins, orc pirates launch raids that are quick, violent, and destructive. They don't want to stay and make themselves vulnerable to a land attack from reinforcements. They want to get in, loot and pillage, and then get out. If they can capture ships that are moored there, so much the better.

Wrecking
She's breaking up! Launch boats and get a-looting!
Morze, Orc Wrecker

Orc flotillas travel far and wide and they have discovered many natural hazards, often at a terrible cost. Pirates know where there are hidden shoals, and dangerous currents, and deadly reefs. When a flotilla comes upon a rich prize that is too fast to catch, one tactic is to drive it towards one of these natural hazards. Once the ship has run aground or been wrecked, it can be plundered by orcs in small boats. Often times, these wreckers will wait on land with their boats, ready to go when a ship founders nearby.

Some sea orcs are not content with using natural hazards to wreck ships; they make hazards of their own! A common tactic is to sink derelict ships in narrow channels, thus blocking them. This actually works better than wrecking a ship on the rocks from the orc point of view, because it can allow the ship to be taken wholesale. Other underwater obstacles can also be created, using rocks, tree trunks, old anchors, and anything else the orcs can find.

ORC VICTORIES

The orcs have marched to war for countless generations. In that time they had their share of victories and defeats. They have made war in every imaginable type of climate and terrain. They have humbled kings and conquered nations. A full history of orc battles would take several volumes and is beyond the scope of this work. Instead this chapter provides an overview of some famous orc victories. These battles show orcish arms in action and provide some examples of how hordes fight.

THE BATTLE OF THE FALLEN CARAVAN

Orcs spend a great deal of time fighting amongst themselves, so the first featured battle is one such encounter between rival warlords. Both Kradush and Ranak were leaders on the rise. Each had defeated several other warbands and added them to his own strength. For a time they kept a respectful distance from each other, but all that changed when a fat human caravan appeared on the steps. It was well-guarded but not enough to stop hundreds of angry orcs.

Kradush caught wind of the caravan first. Within hours his horde was on the march. His wolf archers rode ahead, trying to locate the caravan. This they promptly did, sending riders back to lead the horde to its target. The orcs marched fast, as orcs do, and by the next morning they were near enough to strike. The wolf archers attacked first, circling the caravan and shooting down those humans foolish enough to stand in the open. Then the orc skirmishers came up and added their javelins to the weight of fire. At this point about 20 of the human nomads who had been hired to protect the caravan took to their horses and fled. Most of the wolf archers took off in pursuit, since the caravan had already been stopped in its tracks.

Now Kradush sent in his warrior infantry and that quickly decided the issue. The remaining caravan guards could do nothing to stop the orc warriors from swarming in and hacking them down. Within 15 minutes all the humans were dead and the looting commenced. This would have been the end of the issue if not for the fact that Kradush's rival was lurking nearby.

Ranak had also heard about the caravan and like Kradush he quickly got his horde on the march. When his scouts returned, they reported that Kradush had already taken the prize and was busy dividing the spoils. There was no way Ranak was going to stand for this. His horde was 800 strong and Kradush's only 600. With his blood up and numbers on his side, Ranak decided for an all-out assault. He hoped that a sudden attack with overwhelming force would rout Kradush's warbands in short order. This is not how it worked out.

Kradush was still missing most of his wolf archers, but he posted the few he had in a screen around the battle site. One of these pickets spotted the approaching dust cloud of Ranak's horde and raced back to warn his commander. Knowing that Ranak's horde outnumbered his own, he improvised some defenses quickly. He not only turned the wagons on their sides, but also ordered their horses killed so the corpses could be used as part of the barricades. By the time Ranak's horde arrived, Kradush's warbands occupied a semi-circular defensive work that could not be charged so easily.

Ranak sent forward his skirmishers and archers but they came off worse in the exchange with Kradush's missile troops. The latter had cover and targets in the open. When Ranak's troops came tumbling back, he roared for his warriors to charge. Kradush's missile troops took a fearful toll on the charging troops, as they could hardly miss. Soon enough the warrior infantry charged up to the barricades and a fierce fight ensued. Kradush's warriors beat them off once and then again. Casualties on both sides were high, and numbers were beginning to tell. Kradush could see his quickly shrinking horde might not survive a third charge.

This came in short order and once again battle was joined on the barricades. Ranak's warbands broke through on the east side and then the west. Each time Kradush personally led his guard of great orcs to throw them back and seal the breach.

At this point Kradush's wolf archers returned to the field. Their chase of the human nomads had been long and when it was over they stopped to rest and eat. They came back to find Kradush under siege. It so happened that the leader of the wolf archers was Volog, one of Kradush's most cunning warchiefs. Volog realized that his only chance was to use surprise to his advantage. Although he only had 50 riders with him, he actually split his force in two. One group swept in from the north and the other from the west. They fired their arrows as they charged forward and then, contrary to the usual tactics of wolf archers, they charged in and let their giant wolves attack.

Ranak's horde was entirely focused on swamping the barricades, so these attacks from their rear came as a shock. What's worse, Ranak was one of the first casualties. When he turned around to see what the commotion was, an arrow slammed into his eye and dropped him from his mount. With their leader slain and attacks coming from front and rear, Ranak's horde broke and ran. Many were killed in the rout, and those that were not joined Kradush's horde soon enough.

The Battle of the Fallen Caravan was Kradush's first notable victory but not his last. Volog became a trusted adviser and leader of Kradush's biggest warband.

THE BATTLE OF THE SNAPPING JAWS

The orcs of the Ghoul Swamp spent decades raiding the nearby human lands. Eventually the Toledd Empire conquered this territory and it did not take long for the local governor, Alfonse Falcata, to take exception to the orcs and their ways. He decided he was going to take care of the problem once and for all. He organized a powerful army and led it personally into the Ghoul Swamp to destroy the orcs. "You must destroy rats in their nests," he said at the start of the campaign.

There were local men who advised Falcata against this venture, men who knew the swamp, the orcs, and their tactics. An Imperial army was a blunt instrument ill-suited for this kind of warfare, they argued. Governor Falcata did not listen. The Toledd armies had driven all before them. There was no reason to think it would be any different this time.

Falcata marched his columns into the swamp. They bogged down quickly. The men in their heavy armor were quickly exhausted. The wagons sank into the mire. The supplies grew moldy and inedible. Within a week the army was strung out for miles, mud-covered men struggling to keep moving forward under the eyes of their merciless commander. At this point the swamp orcs struck. Their warlord, Huug, was a master of hit-and-run tactics. His warriors would appear, shower the humans with javelins, and then disappear into the swamp. They attacked up and down the Toledd column and at all hours. Sometimes the orcs carried off human prisoners, and let the screams of these unfortunates taunt their comrades in the dark of the night.

Huug had a flotilla of flat-bottomed boats that he used to great effect. He moved his warbands around with virtual impunity. The Toledd soldiers could never catch them, as the orcs were able to deploy and re-deploy at will. A wiser commander would have realized that the campaign had already failed. Not so Governor Falcata. He could see the orcs taunting him. Always they were just out of reach. If he could just pin them down, he was sure his heavy infantry would carry the day.

Finally it seemed that Huug was ready to engage in a proper battle. Scouts reported the orcs were formed up on a spit of land up ahead. Falcata ordered his men to advance in full armor, despite the heat. The orcs met them with fierce volleys of archery but otherwise stood their ground, waiting for the Toledd charge. As the humans rushed ahead, they made a terrible discovery. The orcs were on dry, higher ground, but the Toledd soldiers had just charged into the wet, muddy ground around it. They quickly mired down and the orcs shot them gleefully with arrows and javelins. Worse was to come. Huug's monster handlers had been hard at work the past week and now their labor paid off. From the flanks of the

human army, giant alligator after giant alligator rose from the water and attacked. They tore into the Toledd line, jaws snapping at their hapless prey.

With the humans in disarray, Huug led his warriors forward. They used long spears and more missile fire to complete the rout of the Toledd army. More warbands in boats appeared on the flanks and continued to harry the humans as they fled. The swamp was littered with corpses, armor, and weapons. The alligators, it is said, never had a greater feed than that day.

Governor Falcata, wounded in the fray, tried to escape on a makeshift raft. He was last seen drifting helplessly through the swamp, his raft covered with hungry, hungry rats.

THE BATTLE OF CRAGNAK'S REVENGE

When Cragnak was young, he was a sworn warlord in the service of Veccetrix, Tyrant of the Seven Flames. Cragnak's horde was but one part of Veccetrix's army and for several years they terrorized the so-called civilized races. It seemed for a time that this dark lord would overthrow the kingdoms of elf, man, and dwarf, but the enemy armies proved stubborn and their commanders resourceful. In the climactic battle of the war, Veccetrix was defeated and slain. Cragnak escaped, but few of his followers did. His horde had faced the high elves of Prince Arlion that fateful day and they had fared poorly. The accurate fire of elven bowmen decimated the orcs' ranks. The charge of their star knight cavalry proved unstoppable. Cragnak and his few remaining followers could do nothing but flee.

The resilient Cragnak returned to his homeland and started again. He had once led a horde but now he commanded a warband at best. Worse than that, he had the stink of defeat on him. No orcs flocked to his banner. He had to fight for new glory and earn new followers. This he did, defeating warband after warband and rebuilding what he had lost. Five years later and Cragnak was a warlord with a mighty horde once again. There are many easier paths he could have trod but he always had a goal in mind: make Prince Arlion and his elves pay in blood for his humiliation.

Cragnak marched into the elven kingdom with 10,000 troops under his command. They made for Eldinur, the prince's city, and cut a swath of destruction through the elven lands. Cragnak believed that Prince Arlion would come out from the city to fight. He would not want his pretty metropolis subject to the ugliness of a siege. In this the orc warlord was entirely correct. Prince Arlion marched out of Eldinur with the elven host at his back.

The elves' chosen point of interception was the fields beyond the village of Torel. There they could anchor their left flank on a river and their right on a small forest. The village, soon crowded with the army's carts and wagons, provided a base to the rear. The day after the elves arrived, their scouts reported that the orcs were approaching. They were making no attempt to skirt around the elves. In true orc fashion, they were coming straight on. Prince Arlion issued his orders and went to bed. He was confident he was going to inflict another stinging defeat on Cragnak.

The elves were deployed by dawn, in case the orcs tried to catch them off guard. Cragnak had no such intention. His army did not arrive in force until 3 p.m. He was content to let the elves stand in their armor under the scorching rays of the summer sun. As the day wore on, the elf units became looser, as soldiers went to get water from the river or sat down to rest. By the time the orc horde came out to fight, the elves were already hot and tired.

Cragnak had put his most aggressive warchiefs and all the berserkers on the right flank by the river. He knew he could not hold them back and did not even try. Shortly after the horde's arrival on the field, the orc right flank surged forward. Hundreds of berserkers stormed ahead, followed by warrior infantry. The elven archers responded with flights of arrows. Dozens of orcs fell but the berserkers were fast. The elf battle line was also still ragged, and it buckled when the berserkers crashed into it. With flailing axes and manic screams, the berserkers drove into the elven lines. Warrior infantry followed them in, trying to widen the breach. The elven spearmen, however, were well-trained. They bowed inward, but their line did not break. They linked shields again and counter-attacked. The berserkers died on the ends of spears or pierced by falling arrows. The warrior infantry retreated after taking heavy casualties. Prince Arlion shifted some troops from the center to reinforce his left, but he was well pleased. The first orc attack had been repulsed.

While that attack was reaching its bloody climax, Cragnak had his ballista brought up on his left flank on their wagons. His skirmishers moved ahead and began firing arrows and javelins at the elven ranks. They were greeted with withering return fire, which Cragnak knew they could not withstand for long. He gave the command, and the ballista began firing war-heads into the enemy battle line. These exploded in the tightly packed ranks and caused scores of elves to fall to the ground coughing. It also disrupted their archery. The orc skirmishers returned to their deadly work. Cragnak followed them up with warbands of warrior infantry and they fought their way deep into the elven lines. The flank teetered on the verge of collapse, but Prince Arlion sent a signal and soon the sound of warhorns filled the air. The star knight cavalry, the pride of high elf arms, charged into battle on their swift steeds. They were a wave of destruction that could not be stopped. They drove their lances home and drove the surviving orcs before them. The elves' right flank was saved

and soon re-established. Once again Prince Arlion reinforced with troops from the center.

By now the sun was setting and the elves had been on the field all day. Cragnak prepared his final stroke. He had tested the right, he had tested the left. Now he would break their weakened center. His instruments for this were now ready for battle: Ironbacks and trolls. He had been thinking about his previous defeat for years. He had been looking to find a way to counteract the elven superiority in archery. Now he would find out if he was right.

The trolls were the point of the spear. They wore heavy armor and carried enormous tower shields. The front rank held these forward as usual, but the rear ranks held them over their heads. Marching with the trolls and underneath these mighty shields were hundreds of goblins with short swords. To the left and right of the trolls, Ironbacks took up a similar formation. Behind them were more warbands of warrior infantry and finally wolf archers.

The trolls and Ironbacks marched forward, slowly and implacably. The elven archers filled the sky with shafts, but their effectiveness was minimal. The shields overhead, particularly the troll's tower shields, provided protection against most of the deadly arrows. The archers redoubled their

effort, but the storm of arrows had little success. The orc attack got within 50 yards of the elven battle line and then charged. Great orcs and trolls smashed through the elven shield wall and drove straight forward. The goblins slipped out of their protective shell and went to work with their short swords. Once the gap was made, warrior infantry swarmed after them, rolling up the elf line to the right and left. Cragnak also leapt forward on his giant wolf, intent on finding Prince Arlion. For his part the prince tried to lead the star knights on another victorious charge, but their horses were blown from their previous attack. The knights were knocked from their saddles and Cragnak found Arlion in the press.

The elves did not wait to discover the fate of their prince. They broke and ran. The wolf archers, unleashed at last, rode after them. Cragnak and Arlion fought on foot, surrounded by trolls already eating the flower of elven knighthood. The prince fought well, wounding Cragnak three times, but the orc's rage could not be withstood. Arlion was too slow in raising his shield, and Cragnak buried his axe in his foeman's head. Meanwhile, the fleeing elves got caught in the village, the streets of which were full of wagons and other transports. The pursuing wolf archers killed hundreds more during the rout.

It had taken many years but at last Cragnak had his revenge.

THE BATTLE OF THE TARNISHED CROWN

One summer day a warband in the service of the warlord Yargut brought a prisoner before him. This human was a tomb robber, and he was taking his latest haul from the mountains to the great trading cities of the east. Yargut asked what he would pay to cross the plains alive. The human offered him a tarnished crown he had found deep under the mountains. It was dented and he didn't think it was worth much. He thought the crown might play to Yargut's vanity and in this he was correct. The thief went on his way and Yargut began to wear his new crown.

Over the next few years the fame of Yargut continued to grow as he won victory after victory and grew his horde. Some began calling him King of the Orcs, since he always wore his "lucky crown" in battle now. Word eventually filtered back to the dwarves of the city of Anved and the consternation there was great. What this orc was wearing could only be the crown of King Vorgil, lost to the dwarves for centuries. Vorgil had taken his closest retainers on what he called "a last great adventure" deep beneath the mountains. None of them returned and his fate and that of his crown remained a mystery.

Siggard, the current king of Anved, sent a delegation to Yargut demanding the crown's return. The orc warlord said the dwarves had lost it and thus had no claim. If they wanted his lucky crown, they could come and take it. Yargut did not think the dwarves would leave their mountains. He was wrong. Siggard mustered his army and marched out to confront Yargut's horde and retrieve the lost crown of King Vorgil. The orc warlord could easily have avoided the fight. Dwarf armies are not known for their speed. Knowing that a victory over the dwarves would enhance his reputation, Yargut moved to meet Siggard's army.

The dwarf army was slow but it was also methodical and had commanders well-trained in military engineering. It only moved 5 miles a day, but always threw up fortifications at the end of the day's march. Siggard knew he could not catch the mobile orc horde, but he hoped to provoke it into attacking him and then break it.

Skarzod, one of Yargut's warchiefs, seemed happy to oblige. He commanded the column closest to the dwarf army. His orders were to keep an eye on the dwarves and wait for Yargut and the rest of the horde to assemble. Skarzod's scouts reported that the dwarf army was 4,000 strong. His column alone had as many troops, so he decided to attack immediately. If he could win the victory alone, he could establish his own horde and serve Yargut no longer.

Skarzod was a fierce fighter but not much of a tactician. He put his cavalry in reserve and then simply charged the dwarf camp. He had contempt for the dwarves and was certain a wild orc charge would carry the day. The dwarves waited behind earthen ramparts as the orcs came on. At long range their ballistas began to fire. These were not the crude ballistas of the orcs, but the height of dwarven craftsmanship. They fired spears at an alarming rate that tore through the orc ranks. Then the dwarves began to shoot with their repeating crossbows. These clever weapons could fire twice as fast as a bow and could punch through armor. This withering fire tore great holes in the orc ranks. The survivors made it to the ditch in front of the ramparts and tried to climb up to get at their foes. The dwarves stabbed down with spears, or fired crossbows at point-blank range. The orc charge was broken and they retreated. Skarzod, increasingly desperate to win before Yargut's troops came up, ordered two more charges. The results were the same. Skarzod's column was decimated.

Yargut arrived in advance of his remaining troops and took in the situation. He did two things immediately. First, he killed Skarzod for defying his orders and getting so many orcs killed. Second, he sent messengers to the other two columns and told them to hold back. He wanted the dwarves to believe that Skarzod's column was his main strength. He had the survivors demonstrate against the dwarf line for the rest of the

day, though he had no intention of attacking. He just wanted to keep King Siggard's attention.

Yargut ordered his other two columns to a lone hill that rose up from the plains about 8 miles away. Their orders were to start digging pits at the base of the hill and then to conceal them. The orcs on the scene did not understand the order but did as they were told. Meanwhile, Yargut had the survivors of Skarzod's column begin a retreat towards the hill the next day. The dwarves scouted the immediate area and found no traps waiting, so they broke camp and followed. They expected an attack that night or the next morning, but it did not come. King Siggard ordered them to continue following the orc trail. This led them to the hill where Yargut's horde awaited.

King Siggard could see warrior infantry arrayed on the hill, so he deployed his army into a battle line. The ballista crews began setting up their weapons but this would take time. Yargut did not intend to give it to them. He sent his light chariots and wolf archers forward to harry the dwarves, followed by skirmishers to add their javelins to the barrage. The dwarves replied with their repeating crossbows and soon the air was full of deadly missiles. The dwarves were well-armored but tightly packed and many arrows and javelins found their mark. Speed was an asset for the orcs but they too took casualties.

Behind this screen of missile troops, Yargut unleashed his masterstroke. The covers were thrown off the pits and out rode a dozen heavy chariots with scythed wheels. The drivers cracked their whips and the chariots moved forward, followed by the warrior infantry from the hill. The wolf archers and light chariots kept the dwarves' attention until the last minute and then rode around the flanks. The dwarves fired their crossbows, but their ballistas were still not deployed. Two chariots were stopped, their wolves riddled with bolts. The remaining ten crashed into the dwarven line, breaking through immediately and causing immense carnage. The warrior infantry followed them in. Fierce hand-to-hand combat ensued. The dwarves used their axes to deadly effect but the orcs outnumbered them. Yargut and his bodyguard rode into the fray, but still the matter was in doubt.

At this point cries were heard to the dwarven rear. It was Yargut's final gambit. He had sent his wolf spearmen on a wide circling maneuver and now they came charging into the vulnerable rear of the dwarf battle line. This decided the issue. The dwarves, ironically enough, were crushed between a hammer and an anvil. Only a few hundred made their way home to Anved and King Siggard was not among them. He had slain many foes but was overwhelmed in the end. The orc warlord took the crown off Siggard's corpse, thus earning the name Yargut Two Crowns.

THE SIEGE OF TRELLOVIR

The Siege of Trellovir is notable for a number of reasons. First, it's a battle that was much longer than typical orc encounters. Second, it involved two orc hordes working together. Third, all of the orcs were in service of a dark elf tyrant.

The dispute that led to the siege did not involve orcs at all. Morrikalli, Tyrant of Kheldrassas, was building her empire and the fortress city of Trellovir made the mistake of crossing her. Morrikalli had conquered several small city states already, and warned that any who took in the refugees would become her enemies. The humans of Trellovir did not want war, but nor could they turn away the ragged survivors of the tyrant's conquests. They prayed Morrikalli would turn her wrath elsewhere, but this was a vain hope.

It so happened that the orc warlord Krugash had just sworn his horde into service to Morrikalli. His forces were also the closest to Trellovir. Morrikalli ordered Krugash to take his horde and storm the defiant city. She did not want a siege. She wanted quick and brutal vengeance on those who dared to defy her. In all, 10,000 orcs marched on Trellovir, ready to carry out her orders.

The orc advance was swift. The columns razed the surrounding villages and drove the survivors inside Trellovir. The Council of Elders that ruled the fortress city was stunned by this turn of events. They thought they would have much more time to prepare for an attack. Nor did they expect that the attackers would be orcs. Suddenly there were thousands of orcs beneath their walls and with them there would

be no parlay.

Krugash had his troops use wood scavenged from outlying settlements to quickly build ladders. While that was going on, the warlord and his scouts assessed Trellovir's defenses. They were considerable. The city was surrounded by a stone wall. Its main gatehouse was to the south, facing the orcs. There were secondary gatehouses to the east and west. Towers and bastions with catapults also pierced the walls. The good news for the orcs was that defenders had had no time to dig ditches in front of the walls. That would make the approach easier, at least.

Krugash split his force into three sections. The smallest faced the south wall and main gate and consisted primarily of missile troops. Their job was to keep up pressure and prevent defenders there from reinforcing the rest of the city. The main effort would be made on the east and west walls. A lodgment on either wall would work, but if both could be carried then the city could be crushed in a vice.

The attack opened with the advance of skirmishing archers. They sent their shafts at the defenders on the walls, while dodging return fire. Trellovir's defenders included a core of professional soldiers and a large number of city militia. Even the latter were well-trained, however, so the archers and crossbowmen on the walls responded with disciplined fire. They also had the advantage of cover, so their losses were few. While the archery duel continued, orc warrior infantry with siege ladders advanced to the walls. Catapult stones gouged great holes in their ranks but they charged forward, set up their ladders, and tried to swarm the defenders. This attack continued for over an hour but in the end it was bloodily repulsed. Defenders threw rocks on the climbing orcs, or dumped scalding oil on them. When orcs did gain the walls, local counter-attacks by the city's soldiers drove them off. With dead orcs and broken siege ladders littering the ground in front of the walls, Krugash ordered the retreat sounded. The first escalade ended in defeat.

Krugash waited for a few days and then tried again. He brought forward his ballistas this time and their gruesome war-head ammunition. He also concentrated the attack on the south wall. This escalade was more successful but failed to break the enemy defenses. The orcs gained the walls in several locations, but an assault by the Knights of the Red Tower sent the orcs tumbling back. These renowned fighters were clad in plate armor and wielded two-handed warhammers and axes. The Knights of the Red Tower were only one hundred strong but their intervention made all the difference. The orcs retreated in disarray.

The day after this assault, the orc horde was surprised by the arrival of another orc horde, 3,000 strong. They were mountain orcs under the command of Vaarg, a warlord from the nearby Blackpeak Mountains. Following close behind Vaarg's horde was another 2,000 troops led by

Morrikalli herself. Her soldiers were experienced dark elf veterans for the most part. However, 150 of them were ogre mercenaries, and these were gladly received by the orcs after their recent repulses.

Morrikalli had a conference of war with Krugash, Vaarg, and their principal lieutenants. After hearing about Krugash's reverses, she decided it would be a siege after all. All the troops began digging siege lines. She also ordered the construction of large mantlets to disguise the mountain orc section of the line from view. These orcs Vaarg set to tunneling. The mountain orcs were experts in this sort of operation and soon several tunnels were snaking towards Trellovir's walls.

Several weeks passed with little activity but the occasional raid from the city, but these were quickly repulsed. A more serious sortie was launched towards the mantlets, but Krugash's wolf spearmen came up from reserve and smashed it before the humans could discover what the mountain orcs were up to. A month after the arrival of Krugash's horde, the third escalade was now ready.

The mountain orcs had by this time undermined a section of the west wall. Wooded supports gave the tunnel structural integrity, but in the middle of the night these were set afire. Over the next few hours all the supports burned away. Shortly after dawn the west wall buckled and then toppled forward. Morrikalli's warhorns blared the attack signal and the combined army began to move. The mountain orcs, delighted with their success, were first to the wall. Warbands of great orcs scaled the rubble and began moving up and down the remains of the west wall. Warrior infantry followed them, some moving into the city itself to spread panic and terror.

In front of the south wall, dark elf and orc archers put up a withering fire. Catapults and ballistas also fired at the defenders. The men on the walls fought bravely but they were outnumbered and they could hear the disaster unfolding to the west. Now the ogre mercenaries came at the south wall with extra stout siege ladders, with Krugash's orcs behind them. The Knights of the Red Tower were the only force that might have stopped the ogres on the wall but they had gone to fight Vaarg's great orcs on the west wall. Some ogres fell, riddled with arrows and burned with oil, but soon they gained the wall. They pulled their clubs off their backs and literally swept the humans off the south wall.

Krugash himself then led his fiercest warband up onto the south wall and then on to attack Trellovir's main gatehouse. Ogres smashed the doors in and then Krugash and his troops rushed inside. The defenders knew that if the gatehouse fell, it was all over for the city, so they fought fiercely. Hundreds of orcs and humans died in the gatehouse, stabbing, punching, and even biting each other in a fight for survival. In the end Krugash could not be denied. He killed every human in the gatehouse and then threw the

gates wide open.

By this point hundreds of mountain orcs were already inside the city. The Council of Elders was desperately trying to contain them with troops pulled from the east wall. With the front gates open, their cause was lost. Thousands of orcs poured into the city and it turned from a battle into a slaughter. The humans had the advantage of knowing the city, but Morrikalli's forces outnumbered them four to one. Soon wolf-mounted orcs were tearing through the streets, slashing down fleeing humans. Cruel dark elves perched on the walls, picking off targets with their longbows. Ogres tore into buildings looking for loot. Morrikalli watched it all from atop the gatehouse, surrounded by the corpses of her enemies. Trellovir had defied her and now it was paying the price. The orcs too had paid a price in this battle, since most of the attackers' casualties came from their ranks. This was of little concern to the tyrant. Her sworn warlords had their uses, but orc losses meant little to her. She rewarded Krugash and Vaarg and began to plan her next campaign.

GLOSSARY

common orc A more muscular average-height orc that makes up the majority of all orcs.

Flesh Eaters The types of horses ridden by orcs, bred by magic over time to become heavy-cavalry beasts that are ridden into battle. Flesh Eaters are the only creatures that can stand to be ridden by orcs.

folklore The unique customs, sayings, stories, arts, and other cultural aspects of a given people.

goblin An aesthetically displeasing sprite creature in fantasy literature, often considered a lesser orc. Or, the smallest of the orc variants.

great orcs Monstrous orcs, over six feet tall on average, that lead most warbands as the strongest and most dominant of the orc variants.

horde A people or tribe of nomadic life, sometimes referring to a large hunting or invading mass. In orc culture, a horde is an orc army, commonly led or organized by an orc warchief or warlord.

shamanism A belief in higher powers, such as gods, spirits, demons, and other creatures that interact only with a shaman; or, a religious authority who is believed to use magic.

Smite-Father The patriarchal god of orc myth who fought alongside the other gods against the titans but, according to orc myth, was tricked to sleep while the other gods divided the spoils of the battle.

warchief The leader of an orc warband, which is usually as few as twenty-five and as many as two hundred orcs, who may become a warlord if successful in enough battles or gaining enough prestige.

warlords Among orcs, warlords lead in both battle and politics, depended on both to fight and to unite orc tribes as the strongest and most influential of their race.

War-Mother A matriarchal god of orc myth who fought alongside the other gods against the titans and declared unending war on the other races and other gods for their slight against the orcs.

FOR MORE INFORMATION

Center for Folklore Studies
The Ohio State University
218 Ohio Stadium (between gates 18 and 20)
1961 Tuttle Park Place
Columbus, OH 43210
(614) 292-1639
Website: https://cfs.osu.edu
Facebook: https://www.facebook.com/CenterforFolkloreStudies
Twitter: https://twitter.com/OSU_Folk
Folklorists and students of folklore are welcome to resources such as an
    archive with more than 12,000 recordings and projects and half a
    century of university research, and to meet with other like-minded
    researchers.

Folklore Studies Association of Canada
CÉLAT - Faculty of Arts
Charles-De-Koninck Pavilion 1030
University of Laval
Quebec City, QC G1V 0A6
Canada
(418) 656-2131, ext. 6607
Website: https://www.congress2017.ca/associations/20
Facebook: https://www.facebook.com/ideas.idees
Twitter: https://twitter.com/ideas_idees
The University of Laval hosts this association for folklore in society and
    literature.

Knight Realms
Website: https://www.knightrealms.com
Facebook: https://www.facebook.com/groups/28680341710
Twitter: https://twitter.com/KnightRealms
The Knight Realms organization provides a place for those interested in
    LARPing (Live Action Role Play) to find others. The organization
    involves live mock combat and social gatherings.

The Los Angeles Science Fantasy Society (LASFS, Inc.)
6012 Tyrone Avenue
Van Nuys, CA 91401
(818) 904-9544
Website: http://www.lasfs.org/index.php?option=com_content&task=vie
w&id=9&Itemid=357
The LASFS is the world's oldest still-active science-fiction and fantasy club,
with meetings, online resources for getting involved, and special events
for members and the public related to sci-fi and fantasy in literature
and culture.

WEBSITES

Because of the changing nature of internet links, Rosen Publishing has
developed an online list of websites related to the subject of this book. This
site is updated regularly. Please use this link to access the list:

http://www.rosenlinks.com/CWAR/Orc

FOR FURTHER READING

Attebery, Brian. *Stories About Stories: Fantasy and the Remaking of Myth.* New York, NY: Oxford University Press, 2014.

Ewalt, David M. *Of Dice and Men: The Story of Dungeons & Dragons and the People Who Play It.* New York, NY: Simon & Schuster, Inc., 2013.

James, Edward, and Farah Mendlesohn. *The Cambridge Companion to Fantasy Literature* (Cambridge Companions to Literature). Cambridge, UK: Cambridge University Press, 2012.

Johnson, Jeffro. *Appendix N: The Literary History of Dungeons & Dragons.* Kouvola, Finland: Castalia House (sold by Amazon Digital Services, LLC.), 2017.

Kushner, David, and Koren Shadmi. *Rise of the Dungeon Master: Gary Gygax and the Creation of D&D.* New York, NY: Perseus Books Group, 2017.

Muhling, Michael. *The Real Middle-Earth: Discovering the Origin of the Lord of the Rings.* Glen Waverly, Victoria, Australia: Sid Harta Publishers, 2013.

Patrick, Den. *Orcs War-Fighting Manual.* London, UK: Orion Publishing Group, 2013.

Sautter, A.J. *Discover Orcs, Boggarts, and Other Nasty Fantasy Creatures* (All About Fantasy Creatures). Capstone Press, 2017.

Simon, Tom. *Writing Down the Dragon: and Other Essays on the Tolkien Method and the Craft of Fantasy.* Calgary, Canada: Bondwine Books, 2013.

Witwe, Michael. *Empire of Imagination: Gary Gygax and the Birth of Dungeons & Dragons.* New York, NY: Bloomsbury USA 2015.

INDEX